D0876019

Christina Aguilera

by Wendy Tokunaga

KIDHAVEN PRESS™

THOMSON
GALE

San Diego • Detroit • New York • San Francisco • Cleveland
New Haven, Conn. • Waterville, Maine • London • Munich

© 2003 by KidHaven Press. KidHaven Press is an imprint of The Gale Group, Inc., a division of Thomson Learning, Inc.

KidHaven™ and Thomson Learning™ are trademarks used herein under license.

For more information, contact
KidHaven Press
27500 Drake Rd.
Farmington Hills, MI 48331-3535
Or you can visit our Internet site at http://www.gale.com

LIBRARY OF CONGRESS CATALOGING-IN-PUBLICATION DATA

Tokunaga, Wendy.
 Christina Aguilera/ by Wendy Tokunaga.
  p. cm. — (Famous people)
Summary: Describes the life and career of popular-music singer Christina Aguilera.
Includes bibliographical references (p.   ) and index.
 ISBN 0-7377-1385-2 (hardback : alk. paper)
1. Aguilera, Christina, 1980– —Juvenile literature. 2. Singers—United States—Biography—Juvenile literature. [1. Aguilera, Christina, 1980– . 2. Singers. 3. Women—Biography.] I. Title. II. Series.
 ML3930 .A36 T65 2003
 782.42164'092—dc21

2002007607

Printed in the United States of America

CONTENTS

Chapter One

A Little Girl with a Big Voice

Christina Aguilera is one of the top female vocalists in the pop music world. She rose to stardom during a time when the number of teen singers was growing. Her mature and powerful voice has been rewarded with fame and success. Her story is of a girl who set her goals early on, worked hard even when things looked bleak, and never gave up until she achieved her dream.

A Passion for Singing

Christina Maria Aguilera was born on December 18, 1980, in Staten Island, New York. Her father, Fausto Aguilera, is an Ecuadorian American; her mother, Shelly, is of Irish descent.

Her father was a sergeant in the U.S. Army, and her mother was a stay-at-home mom. The family was always on the move because her father was transferred to different army bases. Between the ages of two and five, Christina lived in Texas, New Jersey, and Japan. It was a lonely life for the little girl. "I always envied people who had best friends they've known since they were little because I've never had that," Christina says. "I'd have to keep picking up and moving."[1]

It was not surprising that Christina developed an interest in music from an early age. Her mother was a violinist and pianist who spent her childhood performing in Europe. Christina played pretend games of being a famous singer. "I would take a twirling baton and use it as my 'icaphone'—that's what I called it—and lay a towel on the floor as my stage,"[2] she remembers.

Christina loved to perform. She sang to anyone who would listen, sometimes singing out the window to strangers. Her mother remembers three-year-old Christina singing out loud to herself when they rode the bus. People were shocked at the tiny girl's big, rich voice. If a human audience was unavailable, Christina surrounded herself with her stuffed animals and sang for them.

Christina's fourth-grade yearbook photo.

Music Was Comforting

Music also gave Christina **solace** when her parents began to have difficulties

5

with their marriage. "A lot of drama went on in our house. Sometimes you could just feel the tension, like a sensation of verbal violence,"[3] she says. Her parents divorced when she was seven, and Christina put all her feelings and desires into music. Even at this young age she had already decided she wanted to become a famous singer.

When her parents' marriage broke up, Christina's mother took her and her little sister Rachel to live with their maternal grandmother in Wexford, Pennsylvania, a suburb of Pittsburgh. It was there that Christina had her first taste of fame. She started singing at neighborhood parties and then went on to perform at local talent shows, where she often took first prize. People even began to ask for her autograph.

The Verrazano Narrows Bridge connects Brooklyn to Staten Island, where Christina was born.

Christina plays for the camera. She always knew she wanted to be a famous singer.

Star Search

In 1988, when she was eight years old, Christina was a contestant on the TV talent show *Star Search*. Although she was young, Christina knew that winning this competition could be a huge step forward in starting a singing career. She performed one of her favorite songs, which showed the power of her voice: "The Greatest Love of All" by Whitney Houston.

Ed McMahon was the host of Star Search, *the show where Christina Aguilera made her first television appearance.*

Christina gave the best performance she could but lost the competition. Although she was disappointed she did not give up. With her runner-up prize money she bought a portable sound system. The improved sound quality helped her win spots performing at local events, and later singing the national anthem at professional hockey and football games.

The Downside of Fame

After her appearance on *Star Search*, Christina was more of a celebrity than ever in her town, but she learned fame was not all fun. Some people were happy about her progress, but others were jealous. It was difficult for Christina to make friends; a lot of girls were unfriendly because they were **envious** of her success.

Teachers assumed that when Christina missed school, it was because she was busy pursuing her music career. "Sometimes teachers made it difficult because I would be out with the flu, and I would return

Christina became famous in her hometown after her appearance on Star Search.

to school and the teachers would be like, 'Oh, she wasn't out sick; she was out singing somewhere,'"[4] Christina says.

As Christina made more local singing appearances, her social life became harder. At first, she was excited

Christina faced many problems at school with bullies but she stayed focused and determined to succeed.

whenever she was mentioned in the local newspaper, but now it made her worry. Having her name in the paper meant there would be threats from the kids at school who felt that Christina was a snob. Some kids said they were going to beat her up; others said they were going to slash the tires on the family car. Because Christina no longer felt safe walking to school, her mother had to drive her. They made sure to leave the house late when everyone was already in class, to avoid any problems.

The Decision to Move

The stress took its toll and Christina could not sleep well. She began to have nightmares. Her mother decided the family should move to a different town.

Despite these sad times, Christina refused to give up. She worked even harder toward her goal. "I think that's why I became so introverted and focused on my career," she recalls. "You've got to make a decision: Are you going to go down with the situation or are you going to focus and succeed? My dream of being a recording artist kept me going."[5] Although she did not know it at the time, a new opportunity was about to present itself that would make her dream come a little bit closer to reality.

CHAPTER TWO

Big Steps Forward

In 1992, when she was twelve years old, Christina's mother married paramedic James Kearns. Christina gained not only a stepfather, but also two siblings: stepbrother Casey and stepsister Stephanie.

It was also during that same year that Christina auditioned for and won a part on *The All New Mickey Mouse Club*, known as *MMC*. *The Mickey Mouse Club*, created by Walt Disney, had a long history of discovering teen stars.

This was not the first time Christina auditioned for *MMC*. Two years earlier, the show had open auditions in Pittsburgh near where she lived. Christina gave a great performance at the tryouts, but she was not invited to join the show at that time. Although the producers thought she was very talented, they said she was too young. However, two years later, when she auditioned again, the timing was perfect.

Christina was excited to become a part of such a famous television show. She and her mother moved to Orlando, Florida, where *MMC* was taped. Her days were full of rehearsals and dance lessons. "The

Christina demonstrates her powerful voice during a concert.

Keri Russell (center), pictured with the cast of her hit show Felicity, *appeared with Aguilera on the* Mickey Mouse Club.

cast members were chosen to be in certain dance numbers, skits, songs, etc., in a number of ways," she remembers. "It was based on their strongest talents, but also with an effort to spread it out evenly so no one person was doing the same thing over and over. They really worked hard at trying to even it out for all of us."[6]

Christina will never forget her days on the show. "I would sum up my two years on *MMC* as an overall great experience," she says. "I got to learn a lot more about the business, got national exposure, and it helped me mature in a lot of ways. Also, I got to make some wonderful lifelong friends."[7]

MMC Friends

Some of those friends went on to their own great successes. On the show with Christina were Justin Timberlake and J.C. Chasez, who later became members of the boy band *NSYNC. Christina shared a dressing room with both Nikki DeLoach (now a member of the girl group Innosense) and future megastar Britney Spears, whom she used to call "Brit-Brit." Keri Russell (who later went on to star in the popular teen television show *Felicity*) was also a member of *MMC*. "I was very close to Britney," Christina remembers. "She and I were the youngest. We totally looked up to Keri Russell; she was a Barbie doll to us. She was sixteen at the time and Britney was eleven, and I was twelve, and we were both in awe of her. We were always touching her hair. We were such little dorks!"[8]

Christina loved performing on *MMC* and enjoyed being with so many kids who were just as driven toward success as she was. However, after Christina completed her second year on the show, *MMC* was canceled.

Touring the World

Although she was sad about the cancellation of *MMC*, Christina did not sit around feeling sorry for herself. By this time she was fourteen and *MMC* had given her the exposure she needed to move her career along. She recorded a duet with Japanese pop singer Keizo Nakanishi, "All I Wanna Do," and Christina appeared in the video for the song. She also performed with Keizo in two concerts in Tokyo.

Soon after that Christina was off to Europe, representing the United States at a music festival in Brasov, Romania. She performed a two-song set in front of an audience of ten thousand in a concert that also included major stars Sheryl Crow and Diana Ross. Christina put her showmanship to the test. She waded through the huge crowd as she sang, almost causing a riot, as screaming fans pushed forward to get a closer look at her.

"Reflection"

When Christina went back home to Pennsylvania, her manager had news about an exciting opportunity. Record producers at the Disney Studios were looking for a vocalist to record a song called "Reflection." The song was going to be in *Mulan*, an animated movie about a young Chinese girl who disguises herself as a male soldier to save her father from harm. The record company wanted a singer with a powerful voice, and one who could hit high notes.

Aguilera sang at a music festival that also included performances by Sheryl Crow (above).

Christina knew this could be the break she needed. She made a home recording of herself singing to a karaoke version of Whitney Houston's "I Wanna Run To You." Her manager rushed the tape to Disney executives. Christina spent a nervous few days keeping her fingers crossed, but then the call came—they loved it. Only forty-eight hours later Christina found herself in a studio in Los Angeles recording "Reflection." The high notes she belted out in her demo tape changed her life.

Christina never had formal voice lessons, but she worked with a voice teacher for this challenging song. "They brought in a special vocal coach because it was a really hard song with a wide range, and I tell you, it was great!"[9] she says.

A Successful Song

While she was in Los Angeles recording "Reflection," Christina ran into her old *MMC* friends Justin and J.C. (and the rest of *NSYNC) at the RCA recording studio. This was the first time she had seen them since they had performed on the show together. J.C. was especially shocked when Christina told him she was making a record on the same record label. It was a wonderful coincidence.

Mulan was released in June 1998 and Christina was thrilled to hear her voice through the big sound system in the movie theater. The **lyrics** of the song were especially meaningful to her. "The song's theme—the struggle to establish your identity—was something I

*J.C. (far left) and Justin (center), pictured with the other members of *NSYNC, appeared with Christina on the* Mickey Mouse Club.

could really relate to as a teenage girl myself,"[10] Christina says.

"Reflection" reached the top fifteen in the adult contemporary music charts and was eventually nominated for a Golden Globe Award for Best Original Song in a Motion Picture.

Christina was on her way to becoming a star.

Stardom

After the success of Aguilera's recording of "Reflection," her record label and management knew they had a special talent. Ever since the 1950s, when record company executives realized how much money they could make on popular teen singers, they were always on the lookout for young performers. Usually, these singers were known more for their good looks and personalities than their singing ability. Their popularity often faded quickly, and music critics did not take them seriously.

Aguilera was not only young and pretty, but she also had a powerful, mature voice. Her manager and record label thought she might appeal to both teen and adult listeners.

To give Aguilera a more serious image than most teen pop stars, her managers turned down opportunities for her to sing as an **opening act** for teen groups such as *NSYNC and the Backstreet Boys. Instead, they arranged for her to appear at a series of small concerts in nightclubs and hotels in Los Angeles, New York City, Las Vegas, Minneapolis, and Toronto. She

Aguilera's record label wanted her to have an audience made up of both young and mature fans.

Aguilera promoted her hit song "Genie in a Bottle" by performing in a genie costume.

was accompanied only by a pianist. This allowed her to show that she could really sing and did not need to rely on an elaborate stage show or lip synching just as many teen acts do.

Aguilera also made several appearances at Lilith Fair, which had become an annual showcase for women musicians and singers. Teen singers did not normally appear at this concert. Even though Aguilera was not that well known, her performances drew large, appreciative crowds.

"Genie in a Bottle"

During this time, Aguilera had also been busy recording her first album. Like most albums made by teen pop singers, the songs on her album were written and arranged by the record company's songwriters and producers. Being age eighteen and new to recording, she did not have any say as to what she would sing. Nor did she have the courage or experience to write her own material.

One of the songs on the album was called "Genie in a Bottle." Record company executives decided to release "Genie in a Bottle" as a single in the summer of 1999. It was played heavily on the radio and on MTV, and it became an immediate hit. The song stayed at the top spot on the music charts for five weeks in a row.

Aguilera was proud of the success of "Genie," but she was concerned that the song did not showcase her vocal talents as much as some of the other songs on her album. The song was a little too fluffy for her taste.

She longed to sing in a more soulful style. She also wondered about how the song would be interpreted. It had a breathy, somewhat sexy tone and a chorus with suggestive wording that could have been easily misunderstood.

"At first, I was a little afraid that some people might not completely get where I'm coming from—particularly with 'Genie in a Bottle,'" she says. "The song is not about sex. It's about self-respect. It's about not giving into temptation until you're respected."[11]

Going to the Prom

Aguilera was just eighteen when "Genie" was released. Although the music world saw her as a rising star, she still thought of herself as a regular teen. So she was thrilled when her boyfriend invited her to his prom at a high school in suburban Pittsburgh. Aguilera had been home-schooled by her mother when she became too busy with her career. So, she was excited about going to a real high school, even though she would not know any of the kids there. But when she arrived, many of the girls were rude to her, and none of the kids would talk to her. Aguilera could not help but remember those times when she was younger, when other students were so mean because of their jealousy of her talent and success.

When the DJ spotted Aguilera in the crowd, he immediately put on "Genie in a Bottle." As the song played, many of the kids left the dance floor. "It was kind of sad," Aguilera says. "All I want to do is be nor-

Aguilera has experienced both success and hardship.

mal. But really, it's other people who won't let me be that way." [12]

Even now, Christina knows that fame and success do not always guarantee personal happiness. In preparation for one concert tour Aguilera hired a young man named Jorge Santos as one of the backup dancers.

Jorge Santos (left) was hired as one of Aguilera's dancers.
After becoming friends the two fell in love.

While on the road they became friends. As time went
on they fell in love. However, the strain of Aguilera's
stardom and Santos's lesser role as a dancer caused
problems between them. They broke off their roman-
tic relationship but are still good friends. In fact, Santos

gave Aguilera her dogs—two papillons named Stinky and Chewy.

A Spectacular Success

The release of "Genie" was soon followed by Aguilera's first album. It sold a whopping 2 million copies in the first two weeks. A few months later both "Genie in a Bottle" and the album got a huge response in England, too, ensuring her success as an international star.

Aguilera's first album and single were followed by other big hits, including "What a Girl Wants," "I Turn To You," and "Come On over Baby."

Aguilera's fans had shown their devotion to her by buying her records and attending her concerts. And many music critics noted that Aguilera had more talent and professionalism than other teen girl singers including Britney Spears, Mandy Moore, and Jessica Simpson. But Aguilera was often not taken seriously by the music industry. She was criticized for oversinging. Critics said she went overboard by stretching out her notes as a way of imitating singers such as Mariah Carey and Whitney Houston. Many critics felt that Aguilera

Despite her popularity, Aguilera has many critics.

did not yet have the maturity to hold back her vocal acrobatics. She was trying too hard to show off her power instead of concentrating on developing some depth as a performer.

Best New Artist

A certain amount of respect from the music industry, however, would come to Aguilera in February 2000. Not only would she be attending her first Grammy Awards ceremony, but she was actually nominated for two awards. For the Best New Artist award, Aguilera was competing with pop singer Britney Spears, soul singer Macy Gray, rocker Kid Rock, and blues singer and guitarist Susan Tedeschi. For the Best Female Pop Vocal Performance award, Aguilera was nominated for "Genie in a Bottle." The other nominees were Madonna ("Beautiful Stranger"), Alanis Morissette ("Thank U"), Britney Spears (" . . . Baby One More Time"), and Sarah McLachlan ("I Will Remember You").

Aguilera was certain she did not have a chance of winning either award. She figured she was not as well known as the other nominees in the Best New Artist category because her album had been out the least amount of time. She thought that Britney Spears's super success would nab her at least one of the awards. During the week Aguilera had even practiced in front of a mirror putting on a good loser face. When the big moment came to announce the winner for Best New Artist, no one was more surprised than Aguilera when she heard her own name.

Aguilera accepts her first Grammy in February 2000.

"It was an incredible shock for me," Aguilera says of that night. "I was overwhelmed, shocked, and overjoyed all at the same time."[13]

Aguilera lost the Best Female Pop Vocal award to Sarah McLachlan, but was happy with her Best New Artist award.

CHAPTER FOUR

A Maturing Performer

Back when Aguilera's record producers were ready to release her album, they urged her to change her last name to something that sounded more American. They felt that Aguilera would be too difficult for most people to remember and pronounce. However, she refused—she was proud of her Latin roots and did not want to change her name.

"As a child I knew some Spanish because my father would speak it at home and my mother would answer in English," she recalls. "So I can understand the language but, after my parents divorced, I lost much of my **fluency**."[14]

However, Aguilera brushed up on her Spanish. She recorded a Spanish-language album called *Mi Reflejo* (which means *My Reflection* in English) that was released in the fall of 2000. The album eventually won her a Latin Grammy award for Best Female Pop Vocal Album.

This album came out at a time when Latin music was more popular than ever. However, Latin singers such as Ricky Martin, Marc Anthony, and Enrique Iglesias first became popular by singing in Spanish before crossing over to performing songs in English. Aguilera was in the unique position to cross over from

Aguilera performs in Spanish at the first Latin Grammy Awards.

singing in English to singing in Spanish. Her soulful singing style has also brought a rhythm and blues sound into Latin pop music that was unheard of until then. This ensured her an excellent chance of musical success in another market.

Aguilera continued to make hits and win awards. Her duet with Ricky Martin, "Nobody Wants to Be Lonely," went to number eleven on the American music charts and became a worldwide success as well. At the 2001 World Music Awards, Aguilera was proclaimed the best-selling Latin artist in the world.

Still Friends with Britney

While Christina has enjoyed the attention, and the financial and professional rewards of fame, she has also

Longtime friends Britney Spears (left) and Aguilera (right) present an award at the 2000 MTV Awards.

Nicole Kidman and Ewan McGregor perform a song from the Moulin Rouge *soundtrack. Aguilera also sang one of the film's songs.*

experienced the downside. Media reports have described an unfriendly **rivalry** growing between Aguilera and Spears. Although their schedules are hectic and they rarely have the time to see each other, the two say they are still good friends. Aguilera says they may even work together on a project someday.

The two singers appeared together on the MTV Video Awards. "Presenting with Britney at the 2000 MTV Awards was my favorite part of that night. Because we were on the *Mickey Mouse Club* together, we used to be best friends—and it's so weird how our careers have taken us to these places." [15]

Spreading Her Wings

As Aguilera's success has grown so has her desire to have more control over her career. One of the first steps in this direction was her decision to record "Lady

Marmalade," a **remake** of the old Patti LaBelle classic, from the soundtrack of the movie *Moulin Rouge*.

Record executives did not want Aguilera to record this song. They would have been happy to have her continue to crank out typical teen pop tunes such as "Genie," and keep her teen girl singer image going. Many executives in the music industry do not like changing a winning formula as long as it continues to be successful.

"Lady Marmalade" was a song with a tough image; it had a heavy rhythm and blues feel and a mature theme. And Aguilera would not be singing the song alone. She would share the spotlight with Pink, Lil' Kim, and Mya, all singers who were identified with rap and hip hop—not fluffy teen pop.

Pink, Mya, Lil' Kim, and Aguilera (left to right) present an award at the MTV Video Music Awards in 2001.

Wearing her hair teased and curly, Aguilera expresses her individuality at the Blockbuster Awards in Los Angeles.

But with success comes power and Aguilera was able and determined to record this song. And she proved wrong everyone who said it would be a bad career move. "Lady Marmalade" took the music charts by storm, staying at number one for five weeks. It gave the four singers an MTV Video Award for Best Video of the Year, a Grammy Award, and many others. "The girls were great to work with," Aguilera says. "It was like, 'Let's play dress-up for a day!'" [16]

Aguilera's New Look

When Aguilera first started making records, the management at her record company not only decided what she should sing, but also the way she wore her hair, her

After years of work Aguilera has learned to control her vocal range.

clothes, and her makeup. "Everybody wanted their all-American girl," she recalls. "Maybe that's why I'm rebelling!"[17]

Now Aguilera decides what look she will have in concerts, music videos, and photographs. Sometimes her hair is teased, white blond, and curly, and other times her tresses are long, straight, and honey blond. It is all part of her new freedom to express herself.

When Aguilera's grandmother first saw the video for "Lady Marmalade," she was surprised. Aguilera was wearing a fringed bustier, thigh-high fishnet stockings, and lacy lingerie. Her grandmother was shocked at the sexy outfit and how little her granddaughter was wearing, and she did not hesitate to give her comments to reporters. Aguilera did not mind. She calls her grandmother "feisty" and knows how she likes to speak her mind—just like Christina does.

The New Album

Aguilera has produced four number-one singles ("Genie in a Bottle," "What a Girl Wants," "I Turn To You," and "Come On Over, Baby") and has sold more than 23 million records. She is proud of her success, but at age twenty-one, she is taking even more control over her music.

"When you're new to recording and you get signed to a label, people decide what you're going to be, but you're so excited to be doing it, period. Then you realize, 'Man, I don't know if this is what I really want,'"[18] she says.

Aguilera is working hard on a new album, which she hopes will allow her fans to see the artist behind the singer. She is eager to move away from her teen pop star image. She also has taken music critics' advice by toning down her powerful voice. "I'm not trying to do as much vocal gymnastics. Before, to make up for the kind of music I didn't want to be doing, I would over-riff, to prove that I have talent. It was too much."[19]

Personal Songs

On Aguilera's first album, all the songs she sang were written by other people. Now for the first time she is writing lyrics to many of the songs that will be on her new album titled *Infatuation*. The songs are not about genies in bottles, nor are they overly dramatic love ballads. They are personal songs. They express some of Aguilera's deepest thoughts and feelings.

"A lot of my past is in this record," she says. "What I was going through on tour, what's in my head about everything, about my personal life. It's like an open book. A storybook from beginning to end. I'm telling my story."[20]

A song called "Beautiful" is about self-acceptance and being proud of who you are. In the song "Fighter," Aguilera sings about fake friends who talk behind your back. Another song, "Can't Hold Us Down," is about how women should speak their minds. She also plans to do a song by one of her idols, rhythm and blues singer Etta James. Aguilera admires

Aguilera's talent and hard work will keep her successful far into the future.

James's big, bluesy voice and the fact that she has been able to change her musical style over the years.

Aguilera gave a sneak preview of her new album when she sang another new song from *Infatuation* at the closing ceremonies of the 2002 Olympic Winter Games in Salt Lake City, Utah.

The Future

The future looks promising for Christina Aguilera. She has come a long way from the little girl who used a twirling baton as a pretend microphone to sing to her stuffed animals. As she continues to grow as an artist, her talent, hard work, inner strength, and positive attitude are sure to keep her in the spotlight for a long time.

Notes

Chapter One: A Little Girl with a Big Voice

1. Quoted in Laura Jamison, "Heavyweight," *Teen People Weekly*, December 1999/January 2000. www.teenpeople.com.
2. Quoted in Jamison, "Heavyweight."
3. Quoted in Honie Stevens, "She Rocks . . . She Shocks!" *Caribbean World*, Winter 2001, p. 24.
4. Quoted in Jamison, "Heavyweight."
5. Quoted in Jamison, "Heavyweight."

Chapter Two: Big Steps Forward

6. Quoted in "One on One with . . . Christina Aguilera & Her Mom, Shelly," *MMC Online*. www.freepages.tv.rootsweb.com.
7. Quoted in "One on One with . . . Christina Aguilera & Her Mom, Shelly."
8. Quoted in Jamison, "Heavyweight."
9. Quoted in Jamison, "Heavyweight."
10. Quoted in "Christina Aguilera Biography," *1Hollywood*, www.1hollywood.com.

Chapter Three: Stardom

11. Quoted in Larry Flick, "Aguilera's Expanding Beyond 'Genie,'" *Billboard*, July 24, 1999, p. 12.

12. Quoted in Sophfronia Scott Gregory, "Uncorking the Genie: Ambitious and Talented Singing Sensation Christina Aguilera Becomes a Teen Player," *People Weekly*, September 27, 1999, p. 75.
13. Quoted in *Christina Aguilera's Official Website*. (www.christina-a.com).

Chapter Four: A Maturing Performer
14. Quoted in Stevens, "She Rocks . . . She Shocks!"
15. Quoted in Simon Dumenco, "Christina Comes Clean," *Allure*, May 2002, p. 226.
16. Quoted in Dumenco, "Christina Comes Clean."
17. Quoted in Dumenco, "Christina Comes Clean."
18. Quoted in Dumenco, "Christina Comes Clean."
19. Quoted in Dumenco, "Christina Comes Clean."
20. Quoted in Kim Stitzel, "Christina Aguilera: Not Your Puppet," *MTV.com*, February 2002. www.mtv.com.

GLOSSARY

envious: Wanting the same thing or experience as someone else.

fluency: Being able to speak a language smoothly and easily.

lyrics: The words of a song.

opening act: The performer who appears first in a concert.

remake: To make anew or in a different form.

rivalry: Competing with someone.

solace: Something that gives comfort.

For Further Exploration

Books

Jan Gabriel, *Christina Aguilera: Backstage Pass.* New York: Scholastic, 2000. A souvenir scrapbook filled with photos, a biography, and fun facts.

Websites

Christina Aguilera Official Website (www. christina-a. com). All the latest news, photos, her fan club, and more.

MMC Online (www.freepages.tv.rootsweb.com). Information, biographies, interviews, and the latest news on the kids who appeared on *The All New Mickey Mouse Club.*

Yahooligans! Web Celeb: Christina Aguilera (www. yahooligans.com). Includes a short biography page and links to other Aguilera websites.

INDEX

PICTURE CREDITS

ABOUT THE AUTHOR

Wendy Tokunaga is a freelance writer and editor who lives in the San Francisco Bay area with her husband. She has also worked as an executive web producer for two children's websites. In her spare time she writes fiction, studies foreign languages, and sings Japanese karaoke.